Two Wives Ago

Two Wives Ago

Selected Poems

Lewis C. Mainzer

To order additional copies of this book, contact:
Xlibris Corporation
1-888-795-4274
www.Xlibris.com
Orders@Xlibris.com
59843

Contents

III
Decay & Death

IV
Love

V
Scrutiny & Introspection

VI
Words & Books

for

Caden
Edward & Daniel

Author's Note

This book consists of selected poems written from 1963 to 2008. Many of the earlier poems have been revised in the course of compiling this collection, so a chronological presentation would have been misleading. Instead, the contents are grouped into six subject-matter sections. In a few cases, nevertheless, the reader can estimate the time of a poem's origin.

I am indebted to Edward Mainzer and Kevin Chou for essential technical assistance with preparation of the manuscript. I owe thanks to Pat Schneider, who kindly criticized some poems and encouraged me to go ahead with publication. Because she and the recipients of one or another of these pieces over the years have offered kind praise, blame them and my cherished wife's never-failing support for my courage in thrusting this volume upon an unsuspecting world. If the larger public should, as happens, receive my offering with indifference, I will be content that it may serve as a modest inheritance for my dear sons and granddaughters.

I

Politics & War

THE PUBLIC SERVANT

Speak not of God or King or Pope
for none of these will wield the rope
that hugs the hooded victim's neck
as he, despairing, climbs aloft
to test a loop's too little length.
Then fear the humble hangman's strength.
Church might bless or monarch spare
but hangman, silent, scientific,
power perfect to the task,
neither flinches nor relents.
A lowly servant in that hour
exercises ample power.
Precise as law the body leaps,
a snap! another job complete,
he cuts and hauls the docile dead,
then home to beer and beef and bed;
a civic saint, serene he sleeps.
How sure a trust this guardian keeps.

CLEAN HANDS

Double, double toil and trouble;
Fire burn, and cauldron bubble.
Throw in those who, without need,
lead the world to death and rubble.
Boil them well for evil deed.

"Employees must wash hands before returning to work."
Splendid advice for serving well the public.
The President, our top-most employee,
must be seen to scrub off layers of grease
to undo a war unwisely undertaken,
and the former head of Defense must bathe
generously soaked in water and soap,
the Veep will want a steam-bath, sizzling hot
the Finns can teach him to open dirt-clogged pores,
the eminent learned advisor, a foreign policy expert,
must soak in cleansing salts for a substantial session
lasting hours or days, I would suppose.
Will that make each of them clean
smelling sweet as a rose?
Plenty of other public officials, some little known,
are in want of a proper scrubbing
before they return to rule in the name of the people.
There's been much dirty work in the recent past
but washing hands may be the solution at last.
Knowing "clean hands" is the message we ought to send,
Lady Macbeth, ambitious fiend unsex'd,
may have spoken the truth for all of time,
however resistant dirt always proves in the end.
Keep an eye on those who never go to war
nor fixed a head upon our battlements
yet send off others in the name of courage
while dwelling in seated safety, hands unclean.
This is what a sober sanitation sign must mean.

A PECULIAR STORM: WASHINGTON, D.C., 1999

Shut the windows tight,
bar the doors, stuff the cracks,
pull the shades, have flashlights at the ready.
Storm sweeps over us, through the house,
across the buildings and streets,
pouring in the blackness of the night.
Thunder roars, noise without meaning,
threatening acts from an extra-worldly power,
crackles of lightning,
hiss of rain sheets, spitting at humankind,
voices of angry wind.
The sky is ablaze an instant,
the room is afire,
then all is dark as a hidden evil thought,
explosions, calms, menaces, frights,
an awful force's sinister curse of destruction.
None of this is in the world of nature,
this is people's work, human sounds,
passion is the animating charge,
pious politicians are at large.
Every shred of truth/untruth in reach
is offered as a certainty to teach
the most convenient truth embraced by each.
Such is the modest discourse of: impeach.

MONARCHS

The monarch butterfly has come
to rule upon a purple throne
of stately phlox
in palace gardens bronze and green.
No law prescribes what's orthodox,
no guards attend, no horse, no arms,
no peasants cower in their farms,
no blood avenges ancient harms
for this late-summer king and queen.
Their reign is brief, but all serene.
What can such gentle governing mean?

OWENSBORO, KY, AUGUST 14, 1936

20,000 people watch a hanging

Gentle American brothers, when I was a boy
you came together to watch a man swing from a rope.
He was black, which offered, no doubt, a certain sense of release.
Did you come full of awe or in summer picnic joy?
Are we really, as claimed, God's special, beloved folk,
embodying freedom's home and generous increase,
gathered in this land as a beacon of human hope
to teach the world lessons of brotherhood and peace?
Is God a sly creator who loves His little joke?

ATOMIC POWER

Up and atom
human race,
nuclear power
gone astray
may yet erase
in a single day
what's familiar
on earth's face,
destroying life
without a trace.
Sterile clean,
no trace of green
shall then be seen
to mar the dust.
In power trust.

WALLS

Barriers stretching distant with no end
make a wall dividing friend from friend.
Piled stones create a line from earth toward sky,
a brother prison'd each side questions why.
A wall divides in two a gentle plain
whose wholeness still is spoken by the rain.
Barbed fences speak to all alert to hear it
of that which ever harms the human spirit.
Some day perhaps a barrier stone may fall,
a fence may rot, allowing earth to mend,
one day perhaps there will not be a wall.

WAR EXPERTS

I am no warfare expert
just an old fool in motley, remembering,
one who figures that in war
someone gets hurt
or broken, maimed, disfigured
a face, an arm, two legs, an eye and a foot,
or loses a child, a mother, or
someone loved only after death
when clarified by the halo of too late,
and buildings are crushed
sometimes with a person locked underneath
or a small dog or a lifetime's precious memories.
Nowhere now to hide from cold and hunger,
get on the road moving to another nowhere.
I consider all the fathers who cannot come home
and all who would have been fathers
but are spent in lost heroism
or running too slowly or ducking too late,
or plain bad luck, wrong place at the wrong time,
and those who return in body alone,
pale images of what they were
but hardly men to be accounted any more.
So many are given to feed the ravenous fires.
The experts have a politics, a strategy
a clever set of tactics
a sonorous explanation
faith in the long-term outcome, a theory
and numbers about gain and loss.
I have only an old fool's memory
of the last war
and the one before that
and a few before that one.
They made the world safe for war.
Which war was justified
and which not
I leave to the experts
and the diminished kin of those who died.
I do not calculate, I have only memory.

BOYS' GAMES

Was there ever a time when, on balance,
despite whatever was lost,
war was a gain,
a game that somebody won
and worth the cost?
Young men went out on a testing,
daring to prove themselves,
came home drenched in glory and comradeship
or in blood, broken, crippled,
but knowing themselves and proud,
done for love of a cause or a king
or a city or clan or a woman,
real knights, gallant warriors,
heroes such as Homer brought to life,
though many departed this world on the field of battle.
Were there ever such men, such wars, or is it a myth
that boys in battle became men worthy of legends,
immortal though mortal?
A modern war is too well armed,
honed by experts in every art of killing,
thundering purely impersonal death,
inflaming the sky, crushing the earth, searing the sea,
heralded always by such a shattering noise
that it pierces the very heart of Olympian Zeus,
drowning out every intimation of honor.
If peace is no longer admitted even to longing
and war is the only choice,
let's give the game back to the boys
to play with sticks and shouts
and the odd scraped hand or bruised knee,
until mother calls when the sun sinks
and a hot meal awaits at home.
Let no one but the young boys play at war.

II

Nature

LAWS OF NATURE

Whoever gave concave
gave, too, convex
from other view.
Do not perplex
if what is true
should have to be complex.
The simple laws are few
and life must often vex,
so best, until the world is made anew,
admit that man and nature odd behave.

FISH

The fish that swim
within
the smallest tanks,

condemned
to endless circles
in close ranks,

for all we know
from love of life
give thanks.

A WEED

A weed is not a weed
until it's so decreed
by someone with no need
to see it as a flower.
Though naming's in our power,
in a complicated case
it is best that we concede
that a weed is but a flower
that we think is out of place.

IMPERFECT MOON

The moon tonight is imperfectly round,
a little bit squished where an arc should be found.
Is it warning of something that threatens its shine—
a signal the moon is in fatal decline?
Or just a small defect from which she'll rebound,
resuming a truly symmetric design.

AMHERST ELMS, 1970

Disconsolate New England town,
beloved elms are coming down.
With awkward grace they stately prayed
while, underneath, our children played,
they sheltered house and humbled man
yet all the while their limit ran.
Life was not to be forever,
beetle foe has been too clever,
we rallied science, yet we failed,
and deadly fungus has prevailed.
Reduced in stature, now our town
has lost its once majestic crown.

THE RETIRING CAPE

The sea gnaws away at the sandy coast,
the Cape shrinks into the sea,
a process from which there is no escape.
The geezers are populating the Cape,
which proves a gentle and welcoming host.
If sea swallows all, what must be will be:
a Cape-full of ancients, all will be lost.

RAIN

Four days of gray relentless rain.
Will ever we see the sun again?
God promised no more forty days
but who are we to gauge His ways
for we have only a human brain
and cannot know a rule He obeys.
Whatever in comfort the Bible says,
life seems meant for trouble and pain.
The world is washing down the drain.

TWO VIEWS OF RAIN

A city person sees the rain
as spoiler of a city day;
sunshine is the city way.

A country person knows the gain
of driving dryness from the ground;
rainfall is a country sound.

One like me, who's city bred,
then come to life in country town,
thinks twice when seeing rain come down.

First instinct's quickly better led
as irritation turns to pleasure
in the thought of earth-born treasure.

City folks must be misled,
for country love of rain is truer
to nature and to man, the doer.

MID-SUMMER RAIN

Listen, is it what I think I hear?
Shaking the house, a fierce but welcome sound,
an angry rain beat fists on brittle ground,
breaking free from weeks of grim restraint
that made our desperate hopes for green grow faint,
succumbing to a gloomy depth of doubt.
Sparked by fire shooting out in streaks,
heralded by groans across a sky
that let loose pent-up waters of long weeks
and washed away a dusty shroud of drought
that wrapped a world condemned to burial wear,
though quietly reluctant yet to die.
"Never say you stayed my hand," rain cried,
while soaking every thing unhoused outside,
renewing plants that looked as if they'd died,
refreshing what had shriveled in despair
despite our valiant efforts at good care.
Stale, torturing air, death's breath, had tried
but failed to end the life remaining here.
We heard the rain and came outside to cheer.
None but an infant slept,
the world, exulting, wept.

SPRING DEFERRED

We bore the winter very well
but spring delayed was frozen hell,
with storms and ice and glistening snow
borne in on bitter winds that blow
to brittle blue the finger tips
and chafe the hands and split the lips,
while all those weeks we dreamed of sun
to heal us when the winter's done,
foreseeing flower to feast the eye
and warm, soft earth on which to lie
when symphony of birds will sing
return of life in glorious spring.
This tale is one too often heard
pertaining to all hopes deferred:
life often chastens those who trust
yet find their dreams dissolved to dust,
but those who bear a bitter wait,
however long, however late,
if fortunate and faith is great,
may gain what they anticipate:
a gentle breeze, a warming sun,
newborn flowers one by one,
a bird's return when winter's done.

EARLY SPRING: CROCUSES

Throughout a nighttime's chill
they heard the words, "I kill."
The fires of life unstoked,
the early crocuses croaked.

FORSYTHIA BROUGHT IN

Winter's bare sticks, lemon brown
when all of earth's green has gone down
become first flowers of spring;
what seemed so lifeless a thing
shines now forsythia gold
and, shedding all shyness, is bold
in calling out: winter heart, sing!

AMHERST, EARLY MARCH

Snowdrops bloom against the snow;
if courage is needed, theirs will show
tonight;
grape hyacinth, though still in spikes,
will fatten and color as much as it likes
despite the cold, till its lamps are aglow;
lilacs swell in ripening green,
insisting their purple will soon be seen,
though trembling when wind is more than slight
yet defying chilly morning's flow;
the plum-red leaf of columbine
is showing and I call it mine,
a special herald of the spring,
singing a flower I will know,
memory of summer's most delicate sight.
But count no more of a million signs
or jealous winter may return to curse me
and cold and ice may undermine
all hope for flowers and plants and vines.
Be patient, be silent, let promises be
till spring herself, unbound, breaks free.

EARLY APRIL

(for Daniel)

April celebrant of birth:
keep faith, for warmth will stir the earth.
Though now we suffer chill and snow,
fresh green will enter, all aglow—
a testament to spring's true worth.

Be undismayed
by spring delayed
or by the miles
till summer smiles
and summer games are played.

A FALSE WIND

Here's a false wind doesn't frighten me.
It brings a shivering to the naked tree
and plays a flute sound shrilly from the north,
but out of this bravado what comes forth?
It cannot blow the sun away
or make the clouds retreat from play
or keep a softness out of everything.
Deceitful wind will never chase the spring.

EARLY SPRING

Was it only yesterday
my world was full of snow
where now a million daffodils
in sunshine yellow glow.

Why do spirits so delight
at early flowers' show
— and yet our hearts must burst with joy
that so much hope should grow.

APRIL'S WAYS

April first is a day for fooling around
as nonsense triumphs over whatever is sound,
but as April reaches its vibrant fresh-earth end
it has an entirely different message to send.
It calls out softly, as daffodils join to sing:
Blest be the world that yearly gives us spring.

NEW ENGLAND SPRING

An odd New England spring we have
where summer kisses snow.
Did warm winds come before their time
or cold forget to go?
To straddle thus the hot and cold
suggests world's out of joint,
but if it shows we but obey
then nature makes its point.
Spring does not come upon our call
or as a debt that's owed,
but more as blessing, act of love,
a gift on man bestowed.

SUMMER HUMMERS

Hummingbird Moth hovers in flight
at a sturdy red-tipped welcoming flower
pausing to test: is the offering right?

Hummingbird, too, will surely have flown
at a certain appointed visiting hour
to sample a ruby-rich banquet her own.

Bee Balm bursts into annual bloom
boasting magenta's seductive wild power.
Then, sporting a beautiful beckoning plume,

Cardinal flower, brilliant aflame,
rivals Monarda's proudly crowned tower
in answering diners' tasting-time claim.

Here is a place no one ever will mow.
Hummers enchant us, they fly and not-fly
to give us a spellbinding pantomime show,

suspended as still as a prey-watching beast
before sailing on, swift, silent, and shy,
from an instant of dining, a delicate feast,

balancing still, as if on a dare,
fluttering wings beyond speed of the eye.
Bumblebees, too, are having their share.

Summer and garden offer this sight:
flower and flyer in kiss unify,
an elegant lesson in purposeful flight.

WILD ASTERS

Roses of summer, beautifully bred
into perfect shape and shade of red,
are tributes to the cultivation arts,
as is the stately iris, purple gowned,
whose corm of life was settled in soft ground,
and other flowers, each of which portrays
a tribute to the gardener's knowing ways
as architect of sculpted garden bed,
a perfect whole of well-related parts.
These and all that form a garden space,
every inch well plotted, nothing waste,
must signify how well we order nature
to bend to human judgments of good taste.
But what of boldly scattered aster dots,
purple on purple glory in the green,
spilled in pure abandon on a field
with never a thought to circles or to squares,
nor any hint of geometric pride
or parceling out to colors proper shares
to say: behold artistic work of mine,
a miracle that should in awe be seen
for having colored in once barren lots.
No human hand has plotted this design
nor planted these wild asters of New England.
Are we, in truth, the only garden planners,
is there no cunning hand but human hand
to cultivate what was dull wasted land?
Whoever celebrates the gardener's eye
as master of a skill that planned this sight
might, contemplating beauty that's been won,
respect the work, however it was done,
and praise the hand, or chance, that made it right.

NO PRAISE OF VIOLINS

I do not sing a praise of violins
whose more than human tones, by men abetted
make hymns the very gods, who love sweet sounds
find softening to spirits sorely fretted.
The song that stirs my heart from heaviness
comes humbly out of hidden stones and thickets
come out of tune, all artless, unrehearsed.
So moved am I by choir of the crickets.

AFTER AN AUTUMN STORM

The grass is at thanksgiving prayer
for the first good rain of the autumn,
which banished midnight's mildewed air
and gave us a scrubbed-up morning.
The leaves display a diamond dew,
the laurel has brushed its auburn hair,
and wearied last flowers look almost new.
Is such a pretended rebirth really fair?
The breeze is whispering under its breath:
rest gently my children, next comes death.

FROST-SURVIVORS

Through the first October frost
the colors, still flamboyant, hold
in sun-drenched heads
though many are lost
from being chilled or wet-wind tossed,
yet those that live in sheltered beds
had best be told:
you're worth your weight in marigold.

MOVEMENT

They have no toes and they have no feet
but the leaves are skipping across the street—
or so it seems.
How this happens I scarcely know
for they dance as if to a secret beat,
but when I listen I hear the wind blow,
proving music and motion were meant to meet
and the leaves were meant in rhythm to go.
If I could break free from a mood so sweet
that I dwell in spellbound half-awake dreams,
might I, as well, enter into the flow,
absorbed in their dance, making movement complete?

FALLEN LEAVES

The autumn leaves that last I saw
in shimmering tones, evoking awe,
(a vivid shawl wrapped snug around,
burnt orange, yellow, speckled red,
while sunshine splashed from overhead)
have fled the trees to claim the ground.

Near-winter cold and storm came by
to shroud a rainbow treetop high,
and wind reached out to strip trees clean.
Abandoned leaves that will not die
have formed a carpet, set to fly
in search of land where life is green.

Fierce wind and cold and rain declare
each element has done its share.
A palette's subtle pastel glow
no longer reaching for the sky
rewards inspection when, nearby,
we look not upward but below

at painted earth on which we stand,
a blanket loomed of something grand.
Departed rainbow reappears.
The last leaves twirling downward drift,
migration of autumnal gift
whose colors fend off winter fears.

In pause that follows chilling rain
before the winter's piercing pain,
sweet sunshine sings, a fresh breeze plays
a lively tune, a sweet refrain,
for fallen leaves that yet remain,
their eyes aglow, their hair ablaze.

SUN ON SNOW

Sun on snow
darts light to eye
untainted by
earth-color glow.
Pure chips of fire
that, splintering, sing
and, shattered, bring
a million bits
across light years—
a miracle show.
Most burning hot
and chilling cold
in winter love
take mutual hold
and sparks are born
of sheer delight
in nature's flow.
It's good for a sad, cold winter heart
when, listening in a frozen silence,
such beauty is sounded that we know
much music lives within the snow.
Oh, ruthless winter god, relent
and scatter sun when fury's spent.

CHARITY

Bird and squirrel
squirrel and bird
each was named
with a human word
one a beauty, one a pest
but each has nurtured babes in its nest
both alike will come to feed
searching for life-sustaining seed
both come pleading in tree or on land
looking for help from a human hand
Though one is ugly and one is fair
something decrees that both shall be there
One I love, the other I hate,
but if each must battle a winter fate
who am I to discriminate.

SAVING THE INNOCENT

To our door came in winter a cold, hungry beast,
a remnant of cat, an innocent pleader,
a kitten in need of a life-saving feast.
We offered a meal, but she saw beyond that
and managed to stay, once we'd let her enter.
Thus did a kindness of man cheat the winter.

Now in the garden she waits for a bird
whose innocent singing no more will be sounded.
Feathers and blood she will carry in triumph,
"Dead, and I did it!" her unspoken word.

Winter's poor waif has grown sleek and strong,
in summer a killer, a savage at prey.
Who rescued her once, condemns now the songbird,
who caused her to live allows her to slay.

TREE HOUSE ODE

(for E.S.)

This is my ode to a tree house dweller:
Praised be the monkey, our proud precursor
whose way we may follow, though his manners are coarser
than civilized folks are at present allowed.
Better the sky than a dingy cellar
or a dusty street with a bustling crowd
of earth-heavy, down-looking harried poor folks
who may envy the monkey his capers and jokes
as he swings in the trees and cackles with joy
—so we build us a tree house, a retrograde toy,
to be as a monkey, the swinger and yeller,
peering with glee on a world down below.
What is it that you and the monkey know?

NOAH'S ARK

Noah's ark held many a beast
from the greatest and fiercest down to the least;
some could crawl, others could fly,
some lived in a swamp, some in the dry,
and they varied in many another way
yet lived together day after day
through forty days of endless rain
until they saw the sun again.
Or such, I believe, is the Biblical tale
of a boat without engine or compass or sail
that ended up quite by chance where it sat
atop dry land on Mount Ararat.
The moral lesson of the story tends
to be respect for animal friends
who set an example of patience and peace
until granted at last a longed-for release.
May we follow their pattern of mutual love
when terrible tests rain down from above.

LION

The lion is ferocious when need be,
young zebras shudder at his very name
and deer eyes cloud in fear of what they see;
all lesser beasts must slink away in shame.

No pity comes to play when lions stalk
and strike the slowest, weakest in a herd
so fiercely that it fills the world with talk.
Yet lion is not always undeterred:

he fondles baby in a gentle way,
embraces mother lion as a lover,
will snooze in peace beside a whole array
of lesser beasts, while birds go skipping over.

Let him who cannot be all sweetly good
adopt at least the lordly lion's way;
ferocity is but a lesser mood
expressed upon a hunting, killing day.

If truth be told, the beast of prey may pray
his better nature will in time hold sway.

III

Decay & Death

WEDDING GIFT

(for Grand-Mère Safford)

A wedding-given gift I here re-give—
dead husband, aged woman have small needs.
The artist, friend to him who gave the print
in honor of our love-filled marriage day,
was young then, hopeful, but of little fame;
more friendship spoke than price from this sweet gift.
It's worn as well as most of life has worn—
a little faded, yellow-edged and browned.
Capped and girdled, robed and richly bearded,
take old rabbi for your new-formed home;
it makes more sense that he should live with you,
though he fared well in reverent Christian hands.
You hesitate, because of sentiments—
to give away a wedding gift seems wrong?
Have I gone cold, is my old heart ice-bound?
No, memories and love are not extinguished,
but objects have a modest place at best.
I've tidied up in earnest preparation,
till nothing's left but haggard body here,
which once had beauty, now is past such claims.
I strip life bear, I wash my skin, I wait,
till, nothing-fearing, I can look at fate.

THE WISDOM OF AGE

"Sir, how have you lived to a hundred years?"
"No smokes, no women, no whiskey, no beers.
I didn't smoke and I didn't drink!"
"Is that the reason?" "Yes, I think."

"Ma'am, how does it feel now, being alive
to the good ripe age of ninety-five?"
"I ache and forget and I used to sing.
Staying alive is no wonderful thing."

"Tell me, Pops, have you seen great change,
does the modern world seem really strange?"
"Oh, we were hell-raisers when I was a kid,
you'd never believe all the things we did!"

"What is it like, Grandma, dear,
having reached such an age? When I speak can you hear?"
"What's that? I can't hear well at this stage
and I can't read what's on the written page.
I've lost my teeth and my hair is thin
and I barely remember where I have been
and death has claimed most every good friend
and my family has pretty much come to an end.
I'm not proud of living for so many years
and I'm out of hope and finished with tears.
I am out of love and I can't feel rage
and all that I have is the claim of age.
I am what no one should ever desire,
I am ashes remaining after the fire,
a memory left as an action's trace,
a shrunken body and a sunken face,
a broken winner of a meaningless race,
the last survivor of a bygone place.
If I once had purposes, I've lost them all
and am ready to go whenever they call."

"But I see that you still have a clear, sharp mind.
The person I looked for is the person I find."
"The person you looked for has long disappeared
and the prize I have won is the end that I feared.
Old age is not a gold-filled purse,
it's decay and decline and a terrible curse.
But I've spoken enough with a foolish old tongue,
save pity for those condemned to die young,
who hadn't the chance that folks like me had.
For the favor of life, thank God and be glad."

DECLINE

Decay, decline, death's earliest sign
unwelcome guests, must they be mine?
Triumphant faith, a buoyant pride
full strength to act as I design
reluctantly I've set aside
but that need not mean I resign
or seek a space in which to hide.
I cherish self against decline,
more years may yet be justified.

A RESPECTABLE OLD AGE

My plan was gently to settle in and be wise
basking in age's respectable golden glow
but I have been slyly growing a brittle shell
all without formal notice or ceremony,
donning a death mask, trying a grin on for size—
leave ample room for the rattling jaw
leave space for the hollow eyes
let cheeks sink quietly into caves
as the skin flakes off in chalky waves;
the body sinks in silent decay
and the life force slowly fades away.
This is not at all according to plan
and I cannot say when so grave a decline began
or whether I may yet halt its steady march.
Is there a cure that I might improvise?
Am I to be a malevolent Cheshire cat
left at the end with only a grin of surprise?

IN THE PRESENCE OF AGE

In the presence of age, feel a weight of terrible sadness.
Sweet fruit is overripe, gone ugly soft and brown
blind bitch's sagging tumors press her down
the monarch's mind goes batty in his crown
the castle crumbles, emptied of all gladness
the city is a waste beneath the sand
a steeple topples, ending what was grand
a desert settles on a verdant land.
Does nothing lie ahead but pain and madness?
An old man dreams and drips his tears,
I turn my face, averting years.

AGE

Into what confusion has she slid,
or, though unheard, is there an eloquent plea,
a reasoned order that is deeply hid
concerning that which is or yet may be,
to succor her in face of such decay
as breaks the heart of any who still dare
to try to penetrate an opaque wall
that she has built in silence day by day.
Is there sweet memory that days were fair,
evoking still a smile, a single tear,
or only harmonies of empty space, no shape at all,
a swift encroaching tide, the unaware,
which blots out any overwhelming fear,
sustaining through an easy final fall
toward one escape that in the dark shines clear.

WINTER'S CLAIM

Winter is a time for old men's dying.
Is it simply that hearts grow tired of trying
to outwait winter's menacing frost,
or is that they weary of lying,
of pretending a hope that won't appear,
and gain a feeling the dead are near
and the living are almost lost.

CITY DEATH

Beneath a rusting elevated track,
the lifeline of a frantic urban world,
where trains assault, as if by giants hurled,
a building beckons, dressed in sooty black.

Funeral home, a center of calm death,
one would think to find it separated
in a special zone of peace, created
for gently resting those beyond all breath.

What sacrilege to place the body here.
Deafening noise, a periodic roar
conduces ill to saintly spirits' soar
or to sad heartbreak's tributary tear.

Yet it may form a suitable transition.
Who can believe a quiet country hill
would better match a city-dweller's will?
Placement here reflects sound intuition.

Later may he be brought in style to mounds
where grassy meadows shelter him in peace,
but for the moment let the dead not cease
to bathe in city's shrieking, busy sounds.

Tie him to life one hour that he's dead,
till friends accept that peace may now be found.
Then, to harsh praise of city sirens' sound,
march off to country scenes and cut the thread.

DISPOSAL OF REMAINS

Hospital or mortuary
fix 'em up or send to bury.
For the dying everywhere
disposal choices, but why care?
Modern pre-paid crematory
cost efficient end of story,
coffin's dust or ashes urn
each may tempt you in its turn.
Death brings peace beyond all strife,
but, while you can, hold on to life
and, long as you retain a voice,
make the life-affirming choice.
When they say you really must,
choose your form of holy dust.

HARD BARGAINING

May, 1963, Pope John xxiii: "If God wants the sacrifice of
the Pope's life, let it lead to copious favors for the Ecumenical Council,
the Church, and Humanity, which aspires to peace."

The wish came from a dying Pope
that "if God wants the sacrifice"
(his life, that is) it was his hope,
calculating honest price,

that it would lead to "copious favors"
for Church and all of humankind.
He asked not years, yet may behaviors
show a bargaining cast of mind

though nobly pleading for world peace?
Who are we to ask a trade
guaranteeing good's increase
if a compact can be made:

a life to give, a wish to get,
or else postpone the dying
until the day a deal is set
whose terms are satisfying.

Yet what if haggling is the way,
what bargain would I try to strike?
Perhaps to feed the worms one day
as they proceed most workmanlike

and they, in turn, will feed the bird
that lately I at sunset heard.
When my time comes, if it seems fit
and I have courage left for it,

despite the likelihood that fear
will hover as my death draws near,
I may consent to go along
if God will trade me for an evening song.

COMING AND GOING MUSIC

Surely there's music for coming and going.
If offered a choice, I request a hot trumpet
to lead the way downward toward sweet resurrection,
a grand sound, indeed, for return from the dead,
if those who believe it are right after all.
Perhaps an old-timer from New Orleans jazz
may lead us, soul-bursting, in Dixie-land rhythm.
I'll gladly leave heaven (or is it cold grave)
to follow a trumpet returning to earth.
Blow! blow! my rebirth.
But what of my going?
I mean no offense, but a trumpet's not right.
If it is permitted, I'll come calm and gentle
if Andrés Segovia will play me to heaven.
Almost immobile, except magic fingers,
a silver-haired giant
unspeaking, unbending,
who could say no, when his guitar calls.
Purified hearer, I'll enter God's halls.
Segovia going, a sweet trumpet coming,
farewells will be easy, the trip won't seem long.
To heaven and back, I'll be servant to song.

IF I SHOULD LEAVE

If I should leave
my home on earth
please do not grieve—
grief has no worth.
If God permit
I shall return
to teach a bit
of what I learn.
If God forbid
and I must stay
perhaps what's hid
is best that way.

BLEAK DAYS, EARLY WINTER

Early winter, bitter cold,
growth has retreated, no seedlings are seen,
killing frost has blackened the green,
crushing out life that was flourishing, bold

throughout the flower-decked meadow.
Death settles down on our earthly plane,
in spring will plants ever rise again
or is there a never-ending shadow?

What of our friends who weakened and fell?
Called back, we are told, but none of us knows,
except that their presence has come to a close,
wherever beyond us the missing may dwell.

THE TENDERNESS OF SNOW

The snow is resting soft and light
like flakes of stars that drop by night;
if not pure snow, what other sight
so speaks of peace and tenderness.
From silent snow comes trembling sound:
a giant limb white-wrapped around
is hurled by weight from sky to ground.
If innocence can fell a tree,
if strength is hid so cleverly,
who dares to guess what it may be—
in rush of day or sleep of night
forewarned or simply sudden found
in crushing grip or tenderly—
that calls to me, that comes for me.
There is no way one can prepare,
there is no hope that one may dare,
except that it be tenderly.

IN THE DYING WARD

Here in the dying ward
every man is a friend.
If we quarreled long ago
we've all come at last to know
it doesn't count in the end.
We're going the same sad way,
brothers joined by fate
which may come in a week or a day,
so we give such help as we can
to strengthen a failing man,
for we're in it together, mate,
going to face the Lord.
Here in the dying ward.

WHEN THE SNOW COMES

Where will I be when the snow comes?
  Welcoming snow
  warmed by the snow.
Will I be with you in winter?
  No, I must go
  soon I must go
  soothing a sharp hurt
  cooling a fever
  easing a sorrow, a soreness unending
  gaining release from a terrible burden
  into a new home where I may go
  under the gentle good healing of snow.

SLEEP

So sweet is sleep
its calm so deep
its sound a sigh
that if to die
is much the same
by other name
one need not fear
the end, though near.
Why should we weep
when pain will cease
and there is peace
in dreamless sleep.

A LOSS

Earl of Birkenhead (*The Professor and the Prime Minister*) quotes Mrs. Winston Churchill, in a letter of condolence, concerning loss of one's mother: "After that one is nobody's child and it is a lonely feeling."

Now you are nobody's child.
Cleave to whomever you will,
you are bare before winds that chill,
saddened when earth is mild.

Lost is your memory of birth
and the gentlest part of your past.
You are off on your own till the last,
having lain your mother in earth.

BURIAL OF A DAUGHTER

Weep for war's indiscriminate maiming and slaughter,
cry out warning when hate-filled believers come center,
pity the poor who must bear the burden of winter,
beware dread illness from which there can be no shelter,
deep in the bone of age you will certainly suffer
senseless harms that are sent by an evil enchanter
for life is known to be a relentless tormenter,
but pray you may never live to bury a daughter.
Lost, a sweet love and the innocent joy of laughter,
gone, a dear face, now banished to hidden hereafter
—stab in the heart of sorrowing mother and father.
God comfort you, stricken father, desolate mother,
no words can lessen the pain of such a disaster.
God spare us ever having to bury a daughter.

THE ROAD TO PERFECT HAPPINESS

Next door neighbor of my distant, fading childhood,
she, her husband, two kids smashed in a speeding car
en route from North to winter-shunning Florida
long-promised visit to magical Disney World.
I heard the story only second-hand, of course.
What wild anticipation steered them dreaming south
what visions of life-size Mickey Mouse or Minnie
or was it castles or lakes or endless thrill-rides
or color and music or sunshine or escape
what luminous promises lured them on the road
where they sped into a northbound sated pilgrim?
Did the other driver die in a state of bliss
his imagined Disney wonders wholly fulfilled,
did Pat and her kin die at ease in perfect peace
joined in love and hope, celebrating life's sweet gifts?
But such a terrible loss of what might have been
the price of their pursuit of earthly perfection
flying into the jaws of a terrible truth
on the road to a perfect world of make-believe.

CHOSEN SLEEP

If darkness was at last too deep
to bear
so that you gave to endless sleep
your care
and chose it while its shape was yet unknown,
the choice,
though fury-driven, was your own;
your voice
now says what it could never tell,
so deep,
forbidding speech, was your black hell.
Now, sleep.

RESPITE

I

Lord of suffering
Lord of death
Lord of the punishing power
Grant me a week
Grant me a day
Grant me a respite hour.

II

It's time to call a moratorium,
for I have had as much as I can bear:
week on week of being sternly summoned,
as if all other duty's overthrown,
one by one the stately funerals march,
carrying off dear people I have known.
Do I demand too much to ask a rest,
a chance to dwell in calm, to savor life,
to work a while without a coffin's gaze?
Having heard the last macabre jest
and seen the tears, both forced and surely true,
I cry out now: enough should be enough!
I claim the justice of a break from death's
invading my acquaintances and friends.
I need a moment now to draw a breath,
some pause in this parade that never ends.

THE SWIMMER IS SAFE

(for V.H.)

The swimmer has safely reached a distant shore,
beyond the mid-lake island of the pines,
beyond the scissored rocks that cut the calm,
beyond the reach of any summer storm.
No more a speck enfolded in a shadow,
he stretches arms in triumph to the sky,
then, hidden, rests upon a gentle slope
free from every peril of the waters.

The swimmer is safe upon a distant shore,
but we shall never see his face again,
nor feel the strain of distance and of danger,
the test of faith that innocence is safe.
We yearn for a glint of sun, a rhythmic trace,
to watch him match his strength against the water,
to see him rise and stretch against the sky.
We do not know the shore, nor reason why
a certainty he scorned has been imposed,
an empty triumph over cunning waters.

WELCOMING SNOW

The apple tree, old but not wise,
held out its arms to welcome snow,
which, just-right wet and just-right cold,
piled up on limbs grown weak with age;
the main span dropped, no more to rise,
and trunk and branches split apart
crying sounds both sad and savage.
Though it was old enough to know,
the tree put trust too much in snow
and must have died with broken heart.
Or was it so?
Softly snow-covered where it grew,
who can say if perhaps it knew
the risk involved in hosting snow.
A few more years, had they been spent
in fear of winter's element,
would leave to rot a task the snows complete.
The tree did well to greet the executioner sent.

EVEN THE SUN

Even the sun
boast as it may
succumbs at dusk
for it must obey;

moon and stars
renounce their sway
at morning hour
every day;

the great decline
and pass away,
whatever their brightness
none will stay.

THE RULE OF GROWTH

The rule of growth that raises from the seed
a massive oak, from colt a gallant steed,
a mighty person out of infant child,
includes a paradox unreconciled:
in growing strength that shines out every day
from birth itself lies hidden sad decay.

THE END

Cold and snow
ice aglow
that's the way
the world will go
unless it end in heat and flame
which, as for that, is much the same.
We rise above or sink below
and Heaven or Hell is but a name
for life and death's unchanging flow.
A shame, indeed, the world is so
and life is such a losing game
in the only world we will ever know.

IV

Love

TWO WIVES AGO

"She was two wives ago,"
his present wife corrected me
when, having introduced ourselves, I said,
recalling events of forty years gone by,
"Ah, if he is Jonah, then you must be Anna."
But she isn't Anna, she's Elaine,
evidently she's wife number three.
Will they all be buried side by side
in proper order of chronology?
Who will be honored by being put closest to Jonah,
wife number one for being the bride of youthful love,
wife number three for being the devoted caregiver,
the love of age and illness—
we met at a bad time for Jonah, at the hospital,
he and I were room-mates for a day—
or has wife number two a claim I cannot know?
Perhaps she is a saint, too good for any ordinary fellow.
Grown children came to offer bedside comfort
but which wife or wives was mother I never knew
nor whether it leads to special consideration.
Perhaps wives one and two have new companions
for earthly and perpetual consort
and thus no interest in resting forever at Jonah's side.
Wife number one, the Anna I recalled from forty years ago,
came into the room, full of deep concern for the suffering patient,
not a hint of bad feeling among the principals,
everyone on the same side, the side of life and health.
Wife three introduced me, explaining my earlier confusion
with no sense of reproach or embarrassment.
How easy by comparison my life seems, with only wife number one
to snuggle up to me under ground as above.
That's quite a comfort, having chosen well at first.
In wonder at the capacious ways of affection,
I bow before the gods of conjugal love.

DEATH-ROW MARRIAGE

The other day a man on death row wedded,
and just in the nick of time, it would appear,
if marriage is to provide earthly comfort and cheer.
The bride, I assume, could not be lovingly bedded
or caressed affectionately hour after hour.
Such delights of married nights were not within his power,
nor home nor children nor picnics nor walks
nor dancing nor laughter nor long late-night talks.
Then what could such a marriage provide?
Is a moment of chaste affection any kind of solution
to the terrible truth inhering in imminent execution,
to hours awaiting a sign of the dreaded ferryman's ride?
Will an absent wife help him stare calmly at death
as he gasps at the end for a life-saving breath?
Is it better to try to burst the bars and fly off into the night
crying out hatred of justice and of all who dissuade such a flight
to be free, seizing a second of life for all it is worth
or, if it must be too late, at least holding on to hate?
What is the value of peace as reward for embracing one's fate?
Who has come back to tell what he was finally taught?
And the bride, veiled in obscurity, what has she to report?

FIFTY YEARS ARE BUT A NIGHT

A bridegroom drank a wedding toast
that held a magic potion,
and so he slept for fifty years
with scarce a sign of motion
—a flickering of the lids at most,
while sorrowing bride was bathed in tears
for fifty faithful married years.
Friends gathered on the wedding day
when fifty silent years had passed
and, all amazed, they saw the groom
move first an arm, a head at last,
then rise and walk about the room
exuding smiles and gentle sigh
as if a night had just gone by,
not decades of unanswered "why?"
He saw his patient, faithful bride
and went at once to be beside
his wife for life, who stood so near.
She had not lost her beauty's claim
her heart and soul were still the same
her mind and spirit bright and clear,
he called her by her sweetest name
and gently did the two embrace.
Fifty years could not erase
or make affection less sincere.
So let it be with all who love
and hold each other truly dear;
we know their union to be right
when fifty years seem but a night.

A LIFE OF LOVE

What shall we say
a life of love can do?
Observe those who
in unself-conscious daily life convey
the fruit of long affection's gentling way,
the sweet combining work that it has done,
for they are now like one
who once were only two.

LOVE SONG

"How peaceful is the marital bed,"
he smiled but that was all he said
and then, at ease, slipped into sleep
caressing with an arm outspread
while she, replying, stroked his head.
Such is the way when love runs deep,
such is the night old lovers keep.

THE MARRIAGE BED

What got into an old god's head
when he created the marriage bed,
uniting passion and loyalty
alike for peasants and royalty,
for talk, for comfort, side by side,
till both have lived and one has died
and the living somewhat envies the dead
who never need know so lonely a bed.

GRAVESIDE

Woman bent to a rake, tidying earth,
it must seem to you that your toil
in some way sanctifies the soil
when you observe a flower's birth.

Is there a young shoot that you save,
as if its growth could nullify
the judgment: here forever lie,
could free a husband from his grave?

Make soft once more a lover's bed.
In straightening up a twisted flower
you find again life-giving power,
you touch the living, touch the dead.

Sorrow's spent in earthly care,
your work is love, your act is prayer.

STRANGE ECONOMIES

(for Caden)

Shall I earn you with a butterfly
or trade a flower for you in early spring
or rent an hour of laughter from a star that passes by
or walk with you for cost of birds who sing
or barter with an azure summer sky
for share of all the happiness you bring.
How measure what is valued as most high
as if it were a market-centered thing
and not a grace that only love can buy.

CALL TO DINNER

Were I an elegant, expert dancer
I could not move more quickly
or with more grace;
you summon and I answer
obediently, briskly
directly to an accustomed place
ineluctably drawn to that which waits:
hot heaping plates
your welcoming face.

LOVE/BEAUTY

Though love exerts a magnifying power,
pressing claims that mock the test of reason,
it often fades beyond its blooming hour.
Pity a love whose life is but a season,
withering when the birds of autumn fly,
restoring cold proportion to the eye,
wilting worse than beauty of a flower.

THE SNAKE

The snake gave an apple to Eve
and Eve gave the apple to Adam,
then Snake really knew he had 'em.
Next time don't believe
when the snake,
however beguiling, says "Take!"

A MAGIC NAME

We give to a child an enchanted name
to assure a good life and possibly fame
by tricking the gods of chance and fate
who look for persons whose life they may claim
—for all are dependent on what the fates choose.
A magic name for an innocent child
to be nourished in safety, while evil's beguiled.
All we can do is patiently wait
and hope against hope, but often in vain,
as the gods apportion failure and pain
and decide whom to punish and what each will lose.
A magic name to protect one we love
from forces of evil, below or above.
But it never has worked, and we can but wonder
why life tears all of our plans asunder
and will not let us banish chance
or guide the hand of mischievous fate
or see that we live in a dreamer's trance,
until too sorrowed, until too late.
Pity the child with a magic name
whose lifetime of sadness is destiny's blunder
—a sorrow beyond any human blame.

THE FOUR GREENEY CHILDREN

Four fleet runners passing by
not one before the other
but pretty much side by side
waving to me in winter sunshine cheer
bursting as one into joyous carol
in answer to my waving, bell-ringing salute
to celebrate a family home together
celebrating Christmas day.
Daughters and sons lean and strong
all of them graceful runners
running nowhere but for the joy of it
running now with pleasure at being home
remembering perhaps their shared good life
looking each to a future without blemish
confident in their swift limbs
and the kindness of the universe.
That's a sight I will not soon forget.
If time by my command could stop, I'd say, Stop now!
No uphill struggle for these graceful runners
no downhill race with time for shining youths
just flat easy running—smiling, waving
singing together in perfect accord.
Of all moments to bequeath to these good neighbors
this is the gift that I would wish to give.
I'd say, hold at least the memory forever, as I shall do,
knowing we cannot, for even an instant,
hold time still while yet we live.

TREE AND CHILD

I plant a tree to bless a sweet newborn,
as if a lesser life may praise a greater,
in hopes a parallel of growth is drawn
at which to look with satisfaction later.
What if the tree should fall to howling storm
or suffer insects' rot or fatal blight—
ought I not fear to risk a child's own form
by matching him to what might not come right?
No, life's uncertainties can't be undone,
they hover over and within them both—
child or tree may suffer, either one,
each subject to its hidden law of growth.
Shall fear of stunted life mar joy of birth?
I glory in the babe I hold, the tree I set in earth.

WINTER BIRTHDAY

(for Edward)

A winter birthday seems unfair,
with threat of cold and ice and snow
and not a flower anywhere
just when a color guard would show
the world is celebrating too
by letting nature's beauty flow
specifically to honor you.
So be it, we will praise the ice
and claim that snow and cold add spice,
we'll cherish nature's chilly ways
as meant to show you birthday praise.
What nature sends we will embrace
as suited well to time and place:
springtime sweet and summer's heat,
autumn brisk and winter bold—
each marks a day with special grace.
Happy birthday, hot or cold.

TWO MESSAGES FROM THE CAPE

Sarah

Here at Cape Cod
    I hear the sound
of the ocean singing
    all around
and at night
    when the ocean goes to sleep
your ripples of laughter
    are the sound I keep.

Becky

Here at Cape Cod
    I think of you.
The seas are blue
    the skies are blue
the colors are clear
    and always true
and you have
    beautiful eyes of blue.

HONOR TIMELY GIVEN

(for G.S., 2006)

How pleasant is the praise we hear
while upright firmly on the ground
observing sights, absorbing sound
of loving friends all gathered near
to celebrate in amiable ways,
for here is true affection found.
Friends gather for a joyful event
where, joined in heartfelt compliment,
we look upon a radiant face,
gold-bathed in honor, touched with grace.
The briefest celebratory days
outweigh post-mortem's years of praise.

V

Scrutiny & Introspection

A NEIGHBORS' PEACE

Unyoke yourself, my neighbor
who no more intrudes upon a quiet day,
who chose a solemn, solitary way
to shed a burden, flee oppressive labor.

Is it enough that we two simply passed
and neither reached to other at the core
or is it likely that I owed you more,
a word so sweet it succored at the last?

A magic word of truth I might have spoken
if we had talked beyond mundane affairs
to touch a purer vein of human cares,
conjoined to heal whatever's lost or broken.

Was truth too hid for simple eyes to find?
Had something, firing years of simmering rage,
burnt out the heart and cracked its brittle cage
while all before inferno I was blind?

In torment's end let inquisition cease,
together may we find a neighbors' peace.

ANGEL AND SAINT

Piero painted Saint John
halo-enshrouded
bare-footed, bearded
red-robe enfolded
reading a book.
What words do you read, John?
A South German sculptor
no-name forever
or maybe some several
carved, gilded, painted
an angel, full-wingèd
playing a rebec
about fifteen hundred.
Saint John and the angel
are watching my work.
One reads while one fiddles
golden hey diddle diddles
but no noise or glare
(halos blind if you stare)
interrupts the detachment
the calm of these two
unself-consciously posing
a standard of trueness
for all that we do.
Would my own work,
my own spirit's flow,
for even an instant
could breathe of your spirit,
for even a moment
such innocence gain.
Who labors in storms
may labor in vain.

SUM ME UP

Sum me up, sum me up
what do you say?
Forgive me, forgive me
forgive me, I pray.

Balance me, balance me
evil with good,
remember, remember
one time I withstood.

Discover, discover
a kindness I did,
do not, oh, do not
find what I have hid.

Sum me up, sum me up
seeing no sin,
cursèd accountant
implanted within.

IN THE EVENT THAT GOOD INTENTIONS FAIL

Whichever way my life is bent
whatever powerful force is sent
to tempt or to misrepresent
or weaken with a dreadful fear
when pain or threat of death is near,
I hope to live an honorable way
and bring good faith to those most dear
however frail my will may be
whoever judges ill of me
for what I do or what I say.
However far I may decline
forgive me, friends, though fault be mine,
for all my wishes were benign
though actions, failing, went astray.
I did no evil by design.

QUIET

Silence is my spirit's balm
I love the calm.
Yet I can also recognize
the sweetness of a baby's cries
that interrupt my studious ways
disturbing quietest of days
or punctuating nights.
When I am drawn to simple things—
a clock that strikes, a bell that rings
birds' and squirrels' quarrelings
a roaring in the distant heights
an apple landing from a fall
a laugh or whisper that excites,
I hear a voice in calmness call,
"Come, enter life, embrace it all."

I SAW FURTHER

I saw further than you thought.
I saw the moon in a cloudless noontime sky
a blazing sun in a midnight starry field
green hills shining hundreds of miles away
ocean waves touching a city's ancient bay
hidden gems laid deep in the earth
even diamonds and gold
and a small bird soaring to the end of time.
But that was nothing when all is told
and never of special worth.
I saw inside your head
spun through channels in your brain
and out again with your hidden thoughts
which I washed and burnished in a pure spring rain.
You thought I didn't know myself
you saw deeper, you believed, than I could ever do,
a pleasant face on either side shielded a truth unsaid.
Now, though too late to matter, I'll say what I ought,
years ago, living a different moment, to have said:
I have seen further than you thought.

IF THE CACTUS

If the cactus
stony rooted
bristle bearded
bears a flower,
even one
from months of silence,
may not we,
though wasted seeming
through a barren decade's desert,
have been storing, making ready
for a sudden burst of power
in a justifying hour?
If no blossom should embrace
the inexpressive cactus face
is that a proof it lived in vain?
Must every plant have one bright hour
marked by brilliant burst of flower?
May not sober, solemn green
rising stately in its place
with no bloom upon its face
also merit being seen,
embodying a special grace?

CAREERS

One wedded words
one dealt in deeds
each served his own
and others' needs
though if we would be wholly true
each readily enough concedes
the noble work he did not do
to weigh against and set beside
a genuine and modest pride
in having seen his own work through.

A MODEST MAN'S OBITUARY

He did no harm
though very little good
or vice versa,
it being understood,
though it offers little balm,
that judgment rests upon
whether you're a praiser or a curser.

THE MAN WHO WAITED TO SPEAK
UNTIL HE WAS CERTAIN

Silent he was
and silent is,
the precious gift
of silence, his.
But now, alas,
we'll never know
if what he thought,
but left unsaid,
was truly so.

PRACTICING SILENCE

In silence chosen
learn a voice
to speak with silence
not of choice.

EARLY MORNING, SILENT FORM

Unseen we see, yet see no breath—
not drawn and let in rhythmic chest
nor sighed nor sucked nor blown nor hissed.
Must sleep so deep be worldly blessed
or, more than rest, divinely kissed?
Does stillness so complete attest
to heat of love or chill of death?

NO ANSWER

I called, but there was no reply
and, quick enough, I wondered why.
Was illness there or even death
or were they drawing sleeper's breath
or caught in bathing, love, or hate,
in solemn word shared mate to mate
or, not desiring to be rude,
simply savoring solitude.
Though lights were glowing all about,
it may well be that they were out.
They answered neither knock nor phone
so where they were I've never known
and it was not for me to know.
May life be better, shrouded so?

A SERVANT OF TRUTH

Did you ever do a harm to serve the truth
and learn too late it wasn't true at all?
The harm then stood unblessed, unjustified.
Though you atoned by deed or self-told promise
or by night-time's inner flagellation,
the kind that scars yet fortifies the pride,
nothing was undone, though angels cried.
We have to do truth's work the best we can,
but when in doubt, or even shadowed certainty,
serve man.

REGULARITIES

The search for uniformities sublime
or mundane fills our little span of time,
but who will speak the beauty of true laws
when truth has scoured clean his clacking jaws?

THE WHALE CARVING

Gray stone well-buffed reflects the sun's least ray,
the curves are true, they curve as creatures do,
the mouth is quick, the eyes would see me through,
the tail would prove its strength in flight or play.

An Eskimo who never will be known,
who may be deep in darkness many ways,
across uncharted distance draws my praise
for cunning in unveiling whale in stone.

An art so eloquent of human mind,
a stone so given life by human hand
in some uncitied cold-encrusted land,
assures we share the voice of humankind.

BOYS IN THEIR MISCHIEF

Ah, boys will be boys in their mischief,
Young men will be men in their strength,
Come, love them for slyness and boldness,
Come, love the young pranksters near manhood.

Last fall did they take the small pumpkins
And knock the great jack from its post?
Such play is the right of young fellows,
A Halloween trick, no way evil.

One winter they smashed the new snowman,
A giant who glistened in pride.
The children sad wept for their comrade,
But sun would have slain him tomorrow.

In summer they snapped the red maple
Which dances in joy with a breeze.
Now mended with art and much loving,
She'll live and grow lacy new dresses.

Oh, boys will be boys in their wildness
And boys will be men very soon.
Forgive them their touch of the savage,
Pray well for the earth they may ravage.

APPLES

Praise apples and what apples make
sauce and salad and apple cake
cinnamon-scented apple pie
apples to bake, apples to fry
apple butter and pudding and jelly
to gladden a weary winter belly
brown betty and tarts and strudel delight
vinegar, cider, and juice glowing bright
brandy, calvados, and plain apple jack
sweet candied apples (a carnival snack)
fresh eating apples, crispy, tart, red
—daily for health, an old proverb said.
With so many pleasures and such varied use
why mention a single Edenic abuse.

SORROWS

I

The sadness of
the smallest sorrows
will
in time, perhaps
weigh up enough
to kill.

II

If lesser sorrows
by attrition
fail
despite malign intent,
greater ones may lurk
and yet prevail.

III

Sorrows borne
may teach us
if we care
how great a load
of life
we yet can bear.

VI

Words & Books

GOOD FENCES

I often encounter people
—not evil, but half-way readers—
who believe that Robert Frost teaches:
good fences make good neighbors.
The morning paper almost daily reports
an outbreak, one place or another,
of deadly serious fence-making:
the Israelis to keep out terrorists or Palestinians,
a proposal in Congress to wall off the endangered Southwest
to cut off the illegals or the Mexicans
or whoever crosses the river or walks through the desert
in that distant part of the country.
The President has a plan
(it connects with his plan to make the world safe)
to let people come in to work for six years at low wages
then send them home (rich!) and let their cousins come in.
A "win-win" situation he tells us; can't argue with that.
At the airport now there's a human fence:
neatly uniformed guards scrutinize me for bombs or scissors
or perhaps a nail file or other weapon of mass destruction.
I once saw a man in a wheelchair who couldn't walk or speak,
he had a tough time proving his innocence
to get through a phalanx of guards onto a plane for Chicago.
I looked to see if he had shifty eyes
—I think that's what Homeland Security said to do—
but saw only tears of frustration.
Perhaps they train terrorists to weep that way.
I hope to walk the entire GreatWall of China
before, to reclaim the stones, it is disassembled.
A friend of mine has a chunk of the Berlin wall.
Poets make the most impervious fences.
They toss around metaphors,
build turrets of imagination from which to pour boiling oil
onto pedestrian archers squinting below.

They are makers of subtle images,
insinuators of classical references and nods to other poets,
depositors of hidden meanings
buried like gold coins or land mines,
intended only for special persons to find.
They build walls of obscurity a hundred feet high.
Poets know how to keep out the unwanted,
those without requisite training or a well-tuned ear,
too old or young, too dull, too earnest,
too busy with bawling babies or money-grubbing,
listening for easy rhymes and simple meters,
straightforward answers to questions even they could have posed.
The poets could teach the politicians and soldiers
a thing or two about the building of fences.

WORDS' WORTH

Words worth less than Wordsworth's words
may yet at a certain moment shine
though they be poorly poetic made,
seeming weakly to combine.
If words come from an honest heart
tempered by cool discipline of thought
they may join sense and rhythm as they ought,
combining well enough so that they aid
a modest poetry to make a start,
a word-game with ambitions toward an art,
a joyful music, even if ill sung,
hiding perhaps one jewel midst the dung.
If "The Child is father to the Man,"
rhyme happily into age as best you can
renouncing every desire for fame on earth,
playing the game of words for all it's worth.

ROBERT FRANCIS, POET

Robert Francis
always dances
from among inspired words
that he alone, enchanted, heard.
Now he's traveled till he found
a distant, peaceful hidden shore
on which, in joy, he is at rest
savoring all that he loves best—
or does he sleep in dark surround
within a deep and silent ground,
sentenced there to nevermore?
Is it we who have a choice
to give him still a singing voice?

DEFENSE OF DYLAN THOMAS

If I were Caitlin, would I raise my pen
to cry: It is not true he was so weak!
or would I bid all wretched stain be seen,
and trust the way the words of Dylan speak.

MEANING

What fantastic offspring may there be
from giant root of deeply settled tree
encircling silent stone, fixed in its place,
in perfect form of amorous embrace
so none can doubt the passion of what's done;
but what shape is the child of tree and stone
—so odd that it must always play alone?
Or is the tree's intention quite genteel,
giving warmth and comfort stone can feel,
a strong protective ring and nothing more,
a kindness for which tree is guarantor.
Or is it even less, though not malign,
lacking all intent or subtle sign
—a thoughtless world is simply on display
going about its being every day.
Our active minds insist on sharply seeing
more than simple accident in being,
claiming certain signs of sure intent,
as if each sight needs telling what was meant.
To lend rich meaning to a barren earth
where objects, lacking stories, had no worth
were humans sent.

THE SOUND OF A SENTENCE

Listen to the sound of a sentence.
Life in prison or a death sentence?
No, not that kind,
nothing to do with spitting in the street
or killing your good-for-nothing husband.
Oh! More like threatening to kill the President
because you can't stand his stupid grin,
his muddled mind and too-high self-regard?
No, no, keep the Secret Service
and the FBI and the well-meaning local cops
out of this entirely.
What sentence, then, should I regard?
Why, any sentence that takes you lucidly
from here to there,
that stirs or clarifies,
is beautifully economical or musically beautiful
or wears some other virtue you admire.
But that doesn't include spitting in the street?
Never mind, forget I ever spoke.
But I thought you spoke well
and I was truly listening,
and now I better understand why
the word sententious,
deriving, like sentence,
from the Latin, to feel or think,
signifies, though obsolete, full of meaning or wisdom,
though also it means marked by pompous formality,
so I end up still confused.
Well, I could have spoken of sentences
as declarative, interrogative, imperative, and exclamatory
or as simple, complex, compound, and compound-complex,
but perhaps I'd better not;
suffice to say, *sententia,* from *sentire,*
to discern by the senses and mind, to feel, to think,
is at the root of the problem.

Ah, yes, now I get it,
to feel or think leads to all life's mischiefs,
ending us in prison or in death;
I knew it all along.
No doubt, yet still I would advise you,
in a world where every possession and every person
is only on loan,
listen to the sound of a sentence.

THE BANKER'S FAMILY

The banker had a mean, tight purse,
a miser's name or even worse;
money-mania was his curse.

The banker had a lovely daughter
safe at home, or so he thought her;
very chastely had he taught her.

The banker's daughter dressed in lace
and met the plumber face to face
while he laid plans for her disgrace.

She played the plumber's coupling game,
costing her a maiden's name
as she became a scarlet dame.

Being wealthy's little use
if your daughter's ways are loose
when with a man who would seduce.

It cost the banker public shame
every time the plumber came
with wrenches and his torch aflame.

He'd fix a leak or set pipes right,
as people whispered in the night:
"The daughter's loose, the father's tight."

CONFUSION IN LANGUAGE

If summer falls and winter springs
will birds be hushed while a sycamore sings,
will toads be flying overhead
while stones reply to what is said?
Is this the sort of irregular thing
confusion in language may likely bring?
If so, what's odd may be widespread.

MISUNDERSTANDING

What was the word
never well heard?
Perhaps it was "yes."
He only could guess.
He would not infer
so pleasing a sound
and turning it round
assumed it was "no,"
without being sure,
but fearing it, so
he parted from her.
Was fault in the ear,
an ill-structed part,
or cowardly fear,
a misshapen heart?

A DARK (K)NIGHT

A dark-visaged knight
in the dark of the night
lacking the sun or the moon to give light
took sudden flight
upon a swift steed
and was soon out of sight—
an unexplained deed.
Would he set a wrong right?
or perhaps too much mead
had led to a fight.
Whatever the cause, did the lone knight succeed?
All we can say is his fleeing did lead
to a long, eerie, dark knightless night.

VISION WIDE AND NARROW

If I am one who sees the trees
and not the wood,
if given choice so that I truly could
discern a wider sphere, as one who sees
the forest but not each specific tree,
would panoramic vision be pure gain
or would I lose the feel of each tree's grain,
the love of texture that is granted me.
If I scan not a paragraph, but focus on a word,
I have the joy of savoring each syllable I've heard.

WHEN I LOST MY VOICE

When I lost my voice
I had little choice
but to answer my wife with wig-wags.
How my spirit sags
to recall—memory is not by choice—
when I lost my voice.

I whispered and I croaked
feeling infant-helpless, nearly choked
often times in rage
being locked within a silence cage,
weeks of speechless hours without choice,
when I lost my voice.

When I found my voice
it was not at all by conscious choice.
Sudden as a sunbeam after rain,
unthinking, I could really speak again
with fluency and without fearful dread.
What words of God-praise was it I then said?

Nothing profound, no hallelujah-praise,
no more than talk in husband-wifely ways.
My wife smiled broadly on me when I said,
"Please, dear, may I have a piece of bread,"
sufficient speech that she could well rejoice—
at last I had regained my self, my voice.

FALCON AND RAINBOW

(for J.S.)

Was it sky-built to meet a challenge, done on a dare,
to thrust such a building up and up over a little town,
going twenty-five storeys and more into the air
tall and skinny, bricks and windows galore
(trusting the brick-red bricks would never in spite fall down)
then, being a library, filled with plenty of books,
computers, journals, papers, and people,
especially young people
students scurrying, studying, socializing
alive in a hundred kinds of work and play
from deepest scholarship to a coffee-guzzling café;
and elevators, crucial pumping hearts, up and down all day
punishing people who wait hours (in truth, seconds or minutes);
pity the pain of impatience
as if pushing an innocent button hurried the teasing machines.
It grew from no architectural mischief or sly symbolic play
but a dare to use a specified small, central site
as home to a generous library for present and future
—so up and up seemed the only sensible way.
Pleasing lines running from base to top grace the towering building,
but how simpler a low, wide space would have been
for the cart-steering, book-carrying staff
and the busy back-packed truth-seeking user tribe;
yet, however its shape challenges library common sense,
from its height rise two sparkling marks of pure radiance.
On top, the very top, under an endless sky
nests the falcon,
a good place to give birth, food, and first lesson to babes;
these skilled air-current sailors of the sky must calculate
it's perfect family housing for graceful hunters,
with none to challenge their dominion.
The falcon appears of a sudden, off and coasting in gentle arcs
and, when his serious business is done, home again,
the center holds for these beautiful birds of prey,
their gyre respects the library as a beacon, they hold to the core.

And we below can only look up in awe
as these brave dangerous birds give pride to the building.
Flaming from the crest of the building we may other times see
in one blessed moment, if luck serves us well,
a rainbow arc from the very top
(or is it really miles away and we are tricked by our eyes?)
a rainbow arc, almost too perfect to be believed,
stretching from library crown into unseeable distance
—is it a mile, a continent, a circumference?
The work of a master painter
it graces the library like a benediction.
Falcon and rainbow atop a red-brick building
rising absurdly tall in a little New England town,
who would have believed it possible?
Begun by human thought and hands, finishing touches not ours:
We cannot soar with the falcons,
we are no painters of rainbows.
When nature itself shows signs of bestowing praise,
who are we to mock the vertical ways
of a slender straight-up building touching the sky,
its aims, like the very structure, majestically high.

CHRISTMAS EVE AT THE LIBRARY

for the W.E.B. Du Bois Library,
Univ. of Massachusetts, Amherst

Enter on tiptoes
and hear the noise
of sleeping books
throughout Du Bois
or the rustle of pages all around,
but if you cannot hear a sound
the truth may be hiding from whoever looks,
yet it wants to be found.

THE BOOK-LOVER

A young woman stood at the library door
glaring in rage, vibrating frustration
releasing her anger in fury of pounding
to curse an outrageous refusal to open.
It's locked? I said.
Yes, damnit, the library's closed.
You need to get in?
Yes, it's supposed to be open—I think.
Had she homework to do
a report she's already behind-time in writing
a friend with whom she has promised to study
a video, CD, or journal she needed
some well-hidden fact to find out from computers,
which, it's alleged, link to all human knowledge?
I need a book, she said,
a friend who has read it describes it with passion
the author, I know, has a magical touch
a professor has called it a beautiful classic
here is a book that I really must read
a book that I know I am going to love
and I must read it now, I can't wait any longer.
It was plain to see that she sincerely cared,
she'd such a hunger for the written word,
her reasons were as pure as any gold.
I have a backpack here, she said,
and you've a sturdy umbrella
let's batter down the door and go inside.
She felt so deeply
and with such good reason
that I took a nearby fully-loaded cannon
blasted open the door
helped her find the book
and counted it my good deed for the day.
It's nice to meet on any occasion
a genuine lover of books.